ARK TWAIN

DISCOVER THE LIFE OF AN AMERICAN LEGEND

David and Patricia Armentrout

www.rourkepublishing.com

PHOTO CREDITS: "From Dave Thompson's Mark Twain Collection" Cover; © Library of Congress Title page, pages 7, 12, 15, 17, 18, 21; © Hulton/Archive by Getty page 8; © Louisiana Office of Tourism page 10; © PhotoDisc page 4.

Cover: *Samuel Langhorne Clemens is better known as Mark Twain.*

Title page : *Mark Twain in his later years*

Editor: Frank Sloan

Cover design by Nicola Stratford

Library of Congress Cataloging-in-Publication Data

Armentrout, David, 1962-
Mark Twain / David and Patricia Armentrout.
    v. cm. — (Discover the life of an American legend)
Includes bibliographical references and index.
Contents: Young Samuel — Sam the writer — Work and travel — Riverboat
pilot — Mark Twain — Lectures — Family and celebrity life — Tom and
Huck — Mark Twain's legacy — Dates to Remember.
  ISBN 1-58952-660-0 (hardcover)
  1. Twain, Mark, 1835-1910—Juvenile literature. 2. Authors, American—19th century—Biography—Juvenile
literature. [1. Twain, Mark, 1835-1910. 2. Authors, American.] I. Armentrout, Patricia, 1960- II.
Title. III. Series.
  PS1331.A86 2003
  818'.409--dc21

2003002207

Printed in the USA

CG/CG

Table of Contents

Young Samuel

Mark Twain was born Samuel Langhorne Clemens in 1835. When Samuel was four his family moved from the town of Florida, Missouri to the Mississippi River port of Hannibal, Missouri.

Samuel didn't like school. He often played **hooky**. Instead of sitting in class, Sam ran around in the woods with his friends or explored the river.

Sam the Writer

When Sam was about 14, he became an **apprentice** in a print shop. He learned how to print newspapers.

In 1851, Sam worked for his brother Orion as a typesetter for a Hannibal newspaper. Sam also wrote articles, poetry, and made humorous sketches. Sam signed his work with fake names like "Rambler" or "Grumbler."

Samuel Clemens worked in a print shop much like this.

Work and Travel

Sam spent the next few years traveling and working at newspapers and book publishers.

In 1857, Sam boarded a steamboat for New Orleans. He wanted to go to Brazil and see the Amazon River, but instead he pursued his childhood dream of becoming a riverboat pilot.

Sam traveled and worked in many places.

Riverboat Pilot

Sam learned to **navigate** the Mississippi River. Sam learned every landmark from New Orleans to St. Louis. He memorized sandbars, islands, river depths, and names of towns.

Sam earned his pilot's license in 1859. However, Sam's career as a riverboat pilot ended in 1861 when the Civil War (1861-65) stopped travel on the river.

Sam learned to pilot steamboats on the Mississippi.

Mark Twain

Sam traveled west to the Nevada Territory. He wrote for the *Enterprise* in Virginia City. Sam also went to San Francisco and wrote for different papers there. His stories became well-known on the west coast. Sam began signing his work "Mark Twain." Mark Twain is an old river term that means two **fathoms** (12 feet). This means the water is deep enough for a riverboat. Mark Twain became Sam's **pseudonym**.

Sam worked for the Territorial Enterprise *in 1862.*

Lectures

Sam went to Hawaii on assignment for a paper. When he returned to California he found his writings had become quite popular. He decided to give a lecture about his travels. Sam was nervous at first, but his lecture was a success. Sam spoke about his experiences with wit and humor. People loved him.

Mark Twain's popularity grew as he traveled and lectured across the country.

Family and Celebrity Life

Sam met Olivia Langdon in 1867 and soon fell in love. They married in 1870 and later raised three daughters.

Sam continued to lecture, travel, and write about his experiences. In his lifetime he wrote thousands of articles and more than 30 books. Samuel Clemens became known all over the world as the American **celebrity** Mark Twain.

Twain wrote many of his stories in his study at Quarry Farm in Elmira, New York.

Tom and Huck

The Adventures of Tom Sawyer was published in 1876. The story is based on Sam's childhood experiences in Hannibal. Its sequel, *Adventures of Huckleberry Finn*, is Twain's most famous book. The story is about Huck Finn, a boy who flees his father by rafting down the Mississippi River. Huck meets with good and cruel people on his adventure.

An illustration of Huck Finn that appears in Twain's book

Mark Twain's Legacy

Mark Twain wrote less and less in his later years, but he remained a celebrity. He became well-known for the white linen suit he always wore.

Mark Twain died in 1910. He is remembered for his use of real and colorful language, which described his characters, and his humorous way of poking fun at human nature.

Twain received an honorary degree from Oxford University in England.

Dates to Remember

1835	Born November 30 in Florida, Missouri
1839	Moves to Hannibal, Missouri
1859	Pilots a riverboat on the Mississippi River
1863	Begins signing Mark Twain to his writings and sketches
1870	Marries Olivia Langdon
1876	*The Adventures of Tom Sawyer* is published
1885	*Adventures of Huckleberry Finn* is published
1910	Dies April 21 in Redding, Connecticut

Glossary

apprentice (uh PREN tiss) — someone who learns a craft or trade by working with a skilled person

celebrity (suh LEB ruh tee) — a famous entertainer

fathoms (FAH thumz) — water measurements equaling six feet (1.83 meters) each

hooky (HOOK ee) — not going to school when you are supposed to

navigate (NAV uh gayt) — to travel in a ship or plane using maps, compasses, stars, landmarks, etc.

pseudonym (SOOD uh nim) — a false name used by a person instead of his or her real name

Index

Further Reading

Aller, Susan Bivin. *Mark Twain*. Lerner, 2001.
Pflueger, Lynda. *Mark Twain: Legendary Writer and Humorist*. Enslow Publishers, 1999.
Ward, Geoffrey C. *Mark Twain: An Illustrated Biography*. Knopf, 2001.

Websites To Visit

www.marktwainhouse.org/
www.marktwainmuseum.org/
www.cmgww.com/historic/twain/index.html

About The Authors

David and Patricia Armentrout have written many nonfiction books for young readers. They specialize in science and social studies topics. They have had several books published for primary school reading. The Armentrouts live in Cincinnati, Ohio, with their two children.